MONTREAL EXPOS

BILL SHAW

CREATIVE EDUCATION

Dusty Rusty. Staub was Canada's hero because of hustle like this. (1979)

ISBN 0-87191-866-8

MONTREAL EXPOS

This is the story of the Montreal Expos — the first major league baseball team to play in Canada. The story of the Expos is the story of fascinating men like Rusty Staub, Bill "Stoney" Stoneman, Mike Marshall, Steve Rogers, Gary Carter, Andre Dawson, Tim Raines and many other outstanding players. It is the story of how a single team turned an entire country onto baseball.

No story of the Expos would be complete without a tribute to the incredible city of Montreal.

The city is located on an island in the St. Lawrence River in northeastern Canada. Hundreds of years ago fur trappers paddled to this island to exchange their furs for money and supplies. The little village, then called Mount Real, began to grow and prosper.

By 1900 the village was well on its way to becoming a large city. But something strange happened as the city grew up. Half the people spoke English like everyone else in Canada. But the other half continued to speak French. It sounds unbelievable, but even when you walk down the streets of Montreal today, the road signs are in *both* French and English.

The people of the city may be divided on what language they speak, but one thing they're together on is sports. All kinds of sports — football, baseball, soccer and hockey — they love them all!

The Montreal Canadians are one of the most legendary hockey teams in the world. Many times over the years it has won the Stanley Cup for being the best team in the entire National Hockey League. The Expos, on the

ROGERS' RECORDS
Pitcher Steve Rogers holds every Expos career pitching record except for the number of saves. It is held by Mike Marshall.

Letting loose. Expos hurler Steve Rogers shows winning form in this 1981 contest against the Dodgers.

other hand, have won no baseball championships whatsoever. Still, the Expos fans love and respect their team just as much as the city's hockey fans love and respect the Canadians. This book will show you why.

THE GREAT ADVENTURE

For years, a group of baseball-starved Montreal businessmen had been coaxing Major League baseball to come to their city in Canada. In 1960, the league gave Montreal a minor league team, but the fans didn't support it. They didn't want the minor leagues, they wanted the real thing . . . the big leagues!

It seemed that each time the businessmen asked for a team, they got the same answers back from the league. "It's too cold up there," or "Hockey is number one in Canada, baseball will never catch on."

One day Montreal Mayor Jean Drapeau decided that he had heard enough. He knew in his own heart that the people of his city loved baseball. He knew that they dreamed of having a major league club of their own. So he put together a plan to get them one.

In 1967, the city of Montreal held a gigantic World's Fair, called "Expo '67." Millions of people from all over the world visited the beautiful city of Montreal to see the Fair. When they left the city, most of the tourists had a new appreciation for the city itself.

After the World's Fair, Montreal was viewed by the rest of the world as a great metropolis. For such a city, anything and everything seemed possible. Even a baseball team.

Gary "Big Bat" Carter may be a future Hall-of-Famer.

On a beautiful spring morning in 1968, Mayor Drapeau's dream finally came true when the National League accepted Montreal's bid to join the big leagues. The team would be called — what else — the "Expos," and it would be the first big league club to ever play in Canada. It also became the first team in baseball to have its game-day program printed in *both* English and French!

It was the beginning of a great adventure — one that would see the Expos battle and scrap their way from the position of worst team in the league to one of the very best.

THE LITTLE GENERAL TAKES OVER

The first step for Montreal President John McHale was to find a manager for his new team. McHale was a seasoned old baseball man with 20 years experience. He knew how to find just the right man to lead the new team.

After checking several American cities, McHale finally found the man he was looking for in Philadelphia. His name was Gene "Little General" Mauch.

Mauch had been manager of the Philadelphia Phillies for eight and a half years before coming to Montreal. He was a stern old guy who insisted that his players follow strict rules. There was no fooling around when Mauch was on the field.

Mauch loved to talk. On the field, in the dugout, in the parking lot after practice — you could always find him chattering away to somebody.

Robbing Rusty. Andre Dawson charges in to rob former Expos star Rusty Staub of an extra base hit in 1981 action against the Mets.

The only time anybody can remember Gene Mauch being speechless is the first time he saw Montreal's colorful new uniforms. In those days, baseball caps were expected to be drab and simple. But Montreal had chosen a bright red, white and blue cap that was alive with color. It was obvious that the Montreal owners expected their team to have personality and flare.

Mauch put the Expos' cap on his head and got right to work. Coaches and staff were hired. Jarry Stadium, a rickety old place, was renovated, painted and expanded. The excitement was building fast.

By the time the baseball draft rolled around on October 14, 1968, Montreal was a city that was caught up in baseball fever. Clustered around their radios, the Montreal fans listened intently as their very first big league players were selected . . .

Mike Wegener, Maury Wills, Jim "Mud Cat" Grant, Carl Morton, Jose "Coco" Laboy, Bill Stoneman — round by round the team was put together.

The excitement continued through the fall of '68, as Gene Mauch picked and traded his players. Old-timers and rookies tried out under his watchful eye. On the 22nd of January, 1969, Mauch made his biggest trade of all. This particular player's name was Rusty Staub, but the French-speaking people in Montreal immediately nicknamed him "Le Grand Orange" because of his fiery red hair. In no time at all, Staub would become the Expos' first true superstar.

After a two-day retirement, Maury Wills (30) puts on his uniform again and warms up with his Expos teammates. (1969)

A NO-HITTER THE FIRST MONTH

In April of 1969, the Expos headed to West Palm Beach, Florida, for spring training. Up in Montreal, the stadium was nearing completion, and the entire city was getting ready to greet their Expos. But when the team finally arrived back in town from sunny Florida, they ran into one great big problem.

Snow! That's right . . . even in April a thick blanket of Canadian snow covered the baselines at Jarry Field. Maybe the pessimists had been right. Maybe it *was* too cold in Montreal to play baseball after all.

"No way,," yelled the fans. "Let's shovel off the snow and play ball!"

Rusty Staub warmed things up with a red-hot hitting streak that started on the opening night. Home runs, triples, doubles, RBIs — Staub could hit 'em all. On opening night Staub, Dan McGinn and Coco Laboy all drove homers into the outfield bleachers. Opening night the Expos tallied 11 runs against the New York Mets. And that was just the beginning.

Three nights later, April 17, Bill Stoneman pitched himself into the record books. That night, Stoney hurled a no-hit, no-run game against the Philadelphia Phillies. Imagine! The Expos were less than a month old and already they were pitching no-hitters against the awesome old Philadelphia Phillies.

For Stoney it was a dream come true. As a kid growing up in Illinois, he had pictured himself on a big-league mound, mowing down rank after rank of enemy batters.

Face was an inspiration to young Expos rookies in 1969.

THE PEARSON CUP
The Pearson Cup is awarded to the winner of the annual Montreal-Toronto game.

Now that the no-hitter was actually his, Stoney had no intentions of slowing down. Three years later, he would do it again!

AMERICANS IN CANADA

At first Canada was a strange place to live for most of the American-born players. Because so many of the Montreal fans spoke French, the players used to carry little pocket dictionaries so they could understand what was being said. Rusty Staub felt embarrassed the day he received a fan letter and couldn't read it because it was in French. A group of brand-new players on a brand-new team in a town that didn't always speak English — it all added up to a difficult first year.

Of course, that's how it usually is in baseball. First-year teams don't win too many games, and Montreal was no exception. After finishing the first season with 52 wins and 110 losses, Mauch predicted his boys would win 70 games in 1970. The hard-nosed old guy summed up the season like this: "Oh, sure, we figure to get knocked around pretty often at first. But we'll win plenty of ball games. I was really surprised by the crowds in Montreal (the team drew 1,212,608 its first season). I expected noise. But I didn't expect the games to be so important to them. I really felt touched."

BASEBALL FEVER SPREADS

The next year Mauch lived up to his nickname. The "Little General" held one of the toughest spring training

Bob Stinson closed the door at home in his role as catcher in the '70s.

16

sessions in memory. "I felt like an old sock in a washing machine," grumbled one Expos outfielder. Still, it was just what the Expos seemed to need. The batting got sharper, the pitching improved, and the spirit of the team simply soared.

On the opening day of 1970, veteran pitcher Claude Raymond revved up his tired old arm and kept it revved for the rest of the season. If one of the young Expos pitchers got into trouble, Mauch would simply summon Raymond from the bullpen. Twenty-three times Raymond saved the Expos that year. It would be the best year of his entire career.

Of course, starting pitcher Carl Morton didn't seem to need Raymond's help too much in 1970. Morton, a rookie righthander wound up with an outstanding 18-11 record — good enough to be named the National League's Rookie of the Year. He was also voted the Expos Player of the Year.

The Expos did so well in 1970 that many of the old hockey fans started going to the baseball games. Out at the ballpark the fans would sit in the warm summer sun and cheer for their team. The French-speaking Canadians shouted out "*Vive les Expos*" (long live the Expos) when their team started a rally.

There were many big moments in the 1970 season. Like the time Rusty Staub hit four home runs in a doubleheader against the Dodgers. Or the times Ron Hunt made it to first by failing to get out of the way of an incoming fastball.

Pepe Frias showed swift hands in the Expos infield. (1979)

21-INNING GAME
The longest game in Expos history was against San Diego on May 21, 1977. It went 21 innings. Unfortunately, the Expos lost 11-8.

It seems that Hunt had a knack for getting hit by the pitch. He led the league in that category every year for seven years. Some of the players said he was crazy to step in front of 90-mph fastballs. But Hunt didn't seem to mind too much. He just trotted down to first base, listening to the cheers in Jarry Park. Over his entire career Hunt would get hit a total of 243 times!

By the end of the 1970 season, the Expos had won 73 games and lost 89. Mauch's prediction of winning over 70 games in 1970 had come true. The Expos were definitely a team on the move.

EARNING RESPECT

It was in 1971 that the rest of the teams around the National League really started taking notice of the Expos. Like a crusty Army drill sergeant, Mauch kept his team in line. The discipline paid off, too, as the Expos out-hustled, out-pitched and out-hit some of the best teams in baseball, including the New York Mets, the St. Louis Cardinals, the Philadelphia Phillies and more. In reality, the Expos were the straightest, most disciplined team on the field that year. And respect is something that just naturally comes to such a team.

Rusty Staub, "Le Grand Orange," hit well again in 1971. Already he was Canada's number one baseball hero. On the field, he hit with power and style. Off the field, he was the perfect gentleman. By the end of the '71 season, Rusty had a total of 78 homers and 270 runs in his three years with the Expos.

Wall-banger. Del Unser goes to the wall to snag New York Mets Ed Kranepool's long fly. (1977)

Though the Expos finished with a 71-90 record in '71, Gene Mauch was happy for his team. Sure, they still made their share of errors, but their pitching, fielding and batting were improving — and that was the important thing. "Soon the Expos will be contenders. I can just feel it," he said after the season was over.

"Le GRAND ORANGE" DEPARTS

Just before the start of the '72 season, Mauch shocked all of Montreal when he announced that Canada's hero, Rusty Staub, had been traded away. Sad but true. Staub, one of the most dominant players in Expos history, had been traded to the Mets for Mike Jorgensen, Tim Foli and Ken Singleton.

Actually, the experts agreed that it was a pretty good trade. As the '72 season took shape, Singleton picked up where Staub had left off, winning the hearts of the Expos fans with his powerful hitting and flawless fielding.

Tim "Crazy Horse" Foli moved right in and locked down the shortstop spot.

With Singleton driving in runs, and Foli sparking the double plays, Mauch turned his eye to the pitching staff.

Mike Marshall, a wise old hurler who had come to the Expos in '70, was considered one of the top relief pitchers in the game by '72.

Bill Stoneman threw his second no-hitter on October 2, and the Expos continued to build a winning reputation all through the spring and summer of '72.

No, the Expos didn't win a pennant or World Series

Tough Tim Foli. The Expos shortstop bounces off fence but holds onto ball in 1972 contest against the Phillies.

FOLI HITS FOR THE CYCLE
Shortstop Tim Foli was the first Expo to collect a single, double, triple and home run in the same game.

23

that year, but they did provide the loyal Expos fans with 70 victories and some of the most action-packed games in baseball history.

MARSHALL TAKES CHARGE

From the first day of spring training in 1973, the players could see that Mike Marshall was up to something special.

After working hard all winter, Marshall showed up at camp with more zip on his fastball and more curve on his curveball. Nobody, it seemed, could hit him.

When the season opened, Marshall started off on a hot streak. Batter after batter went down to defeat. Whenever Stoney Stoneman, Steve Rogers or any of the other Montreal pitchers would get into a bind, the fans immediately chanted for Marshall. That season Mike appeared on the mound in 92 games (a team record) and saved 31 games (also a team record).

Yep, 1973 was quite a season. Gene Mauch was named Manager of the Year for leading the Expos to within 3½ games of first place in the Eastern division. Along the way there were plenty of fireworks.

Outfielder Bob "Beetles" Bailey drove in more than 60 runs. Ken Singleton was outstanding down the stretch, robbing batter after batter of certain base hits. Tim Foli surpassed everyone's expectations. And Mauch ... well, all he could do was smile.

"Wait until next year," he said with a gleam in his eye. "These guys are just getting started."

Smiling Ken Singleton roamed the outfield in 1982 — and won the hearts of the Expos fans.

A NEWCOMER WINS MVP

Before the end of 1973, Mauch made a move to bring more power to the Expos lineup. Mike Marshall was traded to the Dodgers for outfielder Willie Davis. Though the fans thought it was a bad trade, Davis proved them wrong.

Willie stepped right into the Expos starting lineup and never looked back. All season long his clutch hits and tricky base-stealing inspired the team. More than once, Davis drove in the game-winning run with a towering late-inning homer. With Davis leading the way, the Expos charged through the 1974 season.

When it was over, the team had set records for hitting, pitching and winning. In 153 games, Davis batted .295, had 48 extra base hits, drove in 89 runs and stole 25 bases. The year ended with the Expos standing at 79 wins, 82 losses — their best season ever.

When the vote was taken for most valuable player, Davis won easily. Nobody could think of a player more deserving than Willie Davis in 1974.

THE REBUILDING YEARS

By 1975, baseball fever was so strong in Montreal that tickets were scarce for most of the home games. It seemed that the whole city wanted to watch the Expos. Not only did the players give 110 percent from the field during the season, but the fans gave 110 percent from the stands. Some people said that the Expos fans were the loudest in all of baseball.

The face on the mound. Bill Atkinson helped anchor the Expos pitching force in 1979.

A LONG, DRY SPELL
The longest losing streak in the team's history is 20 games. From May 13 to June 7, 1969, the Expos did not win a single game.

During 1975 the Expos started on a rebuilding program. Mauch and General Manager Jim Fanning had their own ideas about the "right combination" of veterans and young players, but some of their decisions were difficult for the fans to accept.

In order to make room for younger players, Ken Singleton, Ron Fairly and Willie Davis said good-bye. In their place, Mauch brought two promising rookies up from the Expos farm club. Their names were Larry Parrish and Gary Carter. It was history in the making.

Though Parrish and Carter were just rookies in 1975, they hit like seasoned veterans. Parrish ripped 10 home runs and drove in 65 RBIs his first season. Carter hit a phenomenal 17 home runs and knocked in 68 RBIs.

From the very beginning, Mauch knew that he had a ballplayer of great potential in Gary Carter. The tall, handsome California kid was the talk of Montreal. Carter had a way of making the fans proud of the entire team. In his rookie season Carter was voted into the All-Star game. He was also voted the team's MVP in his very first season.

Because of the rebuilding in '75, the Expos slipped to its worst record in four years. The "Little General" won 75 games while losing 87.

When the season ended, team president John McHale decided it was time for a change. He fired Gene Mauch as manager and replaced him with Karl Kuehl. The reign of the "Little General" was over. After seven seasons with the team, Mauch left with a record of 499 wins and

Larry Parrish hits the deck against the Cardinals. Parrish lofted many homers into the distant bleachers. (1978)

627 losses. More importantly, he left knowing that he had done his part in helping an entire country catch baseball fever.

THE TOUGHEST SEASON

While Americans were celebrating the Bi-Centennial in the summer of 1976, Montreal was going through its most embarrassing season. The eyes of the world were focused on Montreal that summer because that's where the Summer Olympics were being held. The Expos didn't put on a very good show. Even the fans walked out on their team in the summer of '76. Attendance dropped from an all-time high of 1,424,683 in 1970 to only 646,704. Nothing seemed to go right that summer.

The Expos continued to lose, game after game, week after week. Carter dropped from 17 home runs to six. Pitcher Steve Rogers won only seven games while losing 17.

The only two players who really shined in '76 were pinch-hitter Jose Morales and pitcher Woodie Fryman. In truth, the team seemed to miss the "Little General."

The Expos slid downhill so fast in '76 that manager Karl Kuehl was fired in September and Expos scout Charlie Fox was made manager for the last few games. No matter. By then, Montreal was on the road to its worst finish in seven years. They won only 55 games that year, while losing 107. Ah, but even that cloud had a silver lining.

Not Valentine's day. Ellis Valentine (17) got caught for a change between bases. (1978)

A DEADLY ARM **Outfielder Ellis Valentine's arm is considered one of the deadliest in all of baseball.**

WIN STREAK
The team's
longest winning
streak is 10
games. It has
been accomplish-
ed twice, in
1979 and '80.

THE START OF THE BIG TURNAROUND

The year 1977 started off with the big bang for the Expos. President McHale announced that Dick Williams had been hired as the new manager. Williams was a fiery coach who challenged his players, squawked at umpires and won lots of ball games.

In 1972 and '73 Williams had guided the Oakland A's to two straight World Championships. Now he was in Montreal.

To add yet another dash of excitement the Expos now moved into Olympic Stadium — the huge new 60,000-seat stadium that had been built for the Summer Olympics.

With Williams leading the way, the '77 season was the beginning of the Expos big turnaround. One of Williams' first jobs was to put some veteran players on his roster. Before the '77 season started, he had picked up hot-hitting Dave Cash from the Phillies and RBI man Tony Perez from the Reds. These two added much-needed power to the Expos lineup.

Once the season began, Cash, Perez Carter and Parrish all had hot bats. Pitcher Steve Rogers put together one of his finest seasons ever. But the big surprise of the year was the outstanding play of three young Expos — Ellis Valentine, Andre Dawson and Warren Cromartie.

Valentine, a stocky outfielder, had 149 hits and 25 home runs in only his second season. Dawson surprised everybody in his rookie season when he belted 25 home runs and had 72 RBIs. His hitting earned him 1977 Nat-

The one-and-only Dave Cash, a welcome addition to the Expos infield. (1979)

32

ional League Rookie of the Year honors. The runner-up for NL Rookie of the Year was teammate Warren Cromartie. Cromartie had 175 hits and 50 RBIs in his first season.

All through the season Williams worked to blend the deep experience of players like Cash and Perez with the raw power of Carter, Parrish, Valentine and Dawson. Williams was convinced that soon his team would be ready to take a run at the National League Championship.

The Expos tenth year, 1978, opened with high hopes in Florida. Over the winter Williams had picked up left-handers Ross Grimsley and Rudy May to add more depth to his pitching staff.

"Grimsley and May are just what the doctor ordered," Williams said. "With four bona-fide starters, we know we'll be able to win the close ballgames."

With Dave Cash batting .289 at second, Tony Perez holding down first with a .283 average and Gary Carter belting 31 home runs, the Expos had plenty of punch in the '78 season. But the Expos' outfield was even better. Cromartie, Dawson and Valentine were quickly becoming the best outfield in baseball. All the ingredients were there to make Montreal serious pennant contenders. Then bad luck reared its head.

Though the hitting was strong in '78, the pitching seemed jinxed all season. In late July, Rudy May fell and broke his ankle. From then on, the Expos struggled on the mound.

One night in Atlanta the Expos did something that

MARSHALL'S TEAM RECORDS
In 1973, reliever Mike Marshall appeared in 92 games and recorded 31 saves. Both are team records.

Catcher Jose Morales was solid as a rock for the Expos of the late 1970s.

made them forget all their troubles. Against Atlanta, on July 30, the Expos set a team record when they slugged out eight home runs.

But that was one of the few real highlights of the season. When the final game ended, the Expos had racked up a 76 and 86 record, good for only fourth place.

Immediately, the Expos launched a special four-point improvement program. By improving the team's speed, catching, bench strength and bullpen, the Expos felt they could squeeze out more wins. The Expos fans held their breath.

A RUN AT THE CHAMPIONSHIP

In '79, the Expos added pitcher Bill "The Spaceman" Lee and speedster Ron LeFlore to the lineup. These two players were the missing ingredients.

When the season opened on April 19, the Expos were off and running. They won 14 of their first 19 games. By the end of May the Expos led the majors in winning percentage (.750) and were on top of the National League in batting with a .284 team average.

It looked like the championship season the Expos had sought for so long. At the plate the Expos outfield started taking charge. Home run blasts, grand slams, sizzling line drives were just a part of the arsenal that Dawson, Valentine and Cromartie unleashed on the National League.

Bill "The Spaceman" Lee was kind of crazy out on the mound. He'd been known to go out to pitch wearing a

Looks easy. Lefty Ross Grimsley made it look very easy as he fired his third victory without a loss in 1979.

gas mask, coonskin cap or even a beanie. But that didn't bother Williams as long as Lee produced.

Lee lived up to his reputation by having one of his best seasons ever. He went 16-10, had a 3.04 ERA and was even voted to the *Sporting News* All-Star Team for his performance.

Through the long, hot summer the Expos stayed neck and neck with the Pirates. Through August and September they hung on. The fans were going crazy. Finally, they thought, their dream of a championship was about to come true.

Going down the stretch the Expos trailed by only two games. But in the last week of the season the team ran into the red hot Phillies and they faltered. When the final game was over, the Expos had missed out by only two games.

The Montreal fans were disappointed. Never in the team's history had they come so close to winning the division. The 95-65 record was by far the best in the team's history.

IN SEARCH OF A TITLE

Everybody said that the 1980 Expos were a team on the verge of something big. Six of the starting eight players were entering their prime playing days. The lineup featured the best catcher, Gary Carter, and the best centerfielder, Andre Dawson, in the league. Carter had hit 29 homers, drove in 101 runs and won a Gold Glove award in '79. Dawson had batted .308 with 87 RBIs and

A SCHOOL TRADITION Warren Cromartie came from the same college in Miami that produced the Yankees' Bucky Dent and the Rangers' Mickey Rivers.

Swarmin' Warren. It was batting practice, 1980, and Warren Cromartie showed the intensity that helped spark the team.

stole 34 bases the same season. People were calling them the best one-two punch in all of baseball.

Rounding out the Expos powerhouse lineup was Larry Parrish, Rodney Scott, Warren Cromartie, Chris Speier, Ron LeFlore and Ellis Valentine.

The pitching was excellent in '80, too. Any of the first three starters — Steve Rogers, Scott Sanderson and Bill Gullickson — had the arm to win 20 games.

From the first game of the season the Expos were off and running. LeFlore sparked the running game with his wild base stealing. Going down the base path he looked like a blur. By the end of the season LeFlore had 97 thefts, including 22 straight steals without being caught.

Early in the season, on May 10, French-born Charlie Lea became only the third pitcher in Expos history to throw a no-hitter. The French-Canadian crowd cheered especially loud for their hero.

In the first week of September pitcher Steve Rogers beat the Mets, 3-0, to record his 100th career win. The very next night 21-year old rookie sensation Bill Gullickson struck out 18 batters to beat the Cubs 4-2. The 18 strikeouts was a club record and one shy of the National League record of 19 strikeouts in a single ball game.

The rest of the '80 season went the same way. Carter, Dawson, and Valentine powered in the runs. LeFlore stole bases. Montreal starting pitcher, Scott Sanderson, came on strong in the late season and won 16 games.

For the second year in a row Montreal and Philadel-

Speier scores Carter. It was a familiar scene in the rowdy 1981 season.

phia battled neck and neck for the division title. It came down to the final weekend before the race was decided.

But the Phillies roared into town for the second year in a row and beat the Expos twice to win the division. The Expos were brokenhearted. The Phillies would go on to win the World Series.

The playoff games caused an outpouring of attention from fans and media all over Canada. The Expos were the center of attention for the whole country. For that time at least, hockey was the number two sport in Canada.

THE FIRST TITLE

The 1981 season started with fans, managers and players talking about a possible baseball strike. The first strike in the history of baseball.

That didn't slow down the Expos, though. They streaked ahead even though they had lost the quickest man on the team. That's right. In the off season, Ron LeFlore, the master basestealer, was traded to Chicago. Some people said the Expos running game was gone, but then they didn't know about rookie Tim Raines.

"Rock" Raines could run like a gazelle. He stepped right into LeFlore's shoes and took off sprinting. He broke LeFlore's basestealing record when he stole 27 straight times without being caught. Instantly, he became the Expos new excitement. Raines helped the team get off to its best start ever.

But then the bottom fell out. The baseball strike stopped Raines and the Expos dead in their tracks. For weeks

The old and the new. Veteran Woodie Fryman (left) and rookie Bill Gullickson team up in spring training. (1981)

OLD MAN RIVER Woodie "Old Man River" Fryman, 43, ran a tobacco farm in the off-season when not working as one of the Expos' top relief pitchers.

and weeks the players and owners battled back and forth. It seemed to go on forever.

Finally, after days of waiting, the shout to "Playball!" was heard again. The first game was the All-Star Game. Expos catcher Gary Carter proved that night that the long wait hadn't cooled off his hot bat. In the All-Star Game he banged two homers and won the MVP award. The Expos were rolling!

For the third year in a row the Expos and Phillies battled down to the wire for the division title. This time the Expos weren't going to be denied.

With Carter leading the hitters, and Rogers leading the pitching, the Expos went into the playoffs and whipped the World Champion Phillies. For the first time in the history of baseball, the National League Eastern Division Championship was brought north of the border to Canada. *"Vive les Expos!"* Bring on the Dodgers!

The Dodgers and Expos squared off in October to decide on the National League Pennant. It was a see-saw series. First L.A. won 5-1, then Montreal came back 3-0. The series moved to chilly Montreal and the Expos rolled to a 4-1 victory. Back and forth they battled. Carter hit a brilliant .438 to prove once and for all that he was the finest catcher in the game. But the Dodgers came back with Burt Hooton and rookie sensation Fernando Valenzuela to capture the series, three games to two. Once again, the dejected Expos had to settle for second best.

Even though Montreal lost, the Expos fans stood and cheered for their team long after the game ended. The

Stan the man. Hurler Don Stanhouse was a steady force. (1977)

fans were hooked on the Expos. Win or lose, they would always be loyal fans.

THE YEARS AHEAD

So that's the story of the Montreal Expos. It's the story of a team that proved to America that Canadians love baseball, too. It's the story of a ball club that struggled and grew into one of the top teams in the league.

It is the story of men like Gene "Little General" Mauch, Rusty Staub, Dick Williams, Gary Carter and many, many more who fought to bring the fans of Montreal a winning tradition.

Finally, it is story that will get better and better every year. Today, the Expos are on the verge of building a dynasty that could rule over the National League. A dynasty so powerful that one day the team should stand next to the Dodgers, Yankees and Cardinals in the history books.

Watch out for the Expos. They have a team that has all the talent to win the World Series. When they do, and it should be soon, it will be a grand celebration in Canada. "Long live the Expos!" *"Vive les Expos!"*

Pitcher David Palmer had a lot to smile about in 1979.

OVER 2 MILLION In 1980, the Expos drew 2,208,175 fans, their best year ever.

Perez puts one over. First sacker Tony Perez rockets one over the left-field wall. (1978)

Clark Alan
Andy

WITHDRAWN

Date Due

W S JAN 1986 FL X MAR				
W S MAY 1986				
3/26				
J M C NOV 1986				
B T X AUG 1987				
JUL 0 9 1987				
JUL 2 0 1987				

Cat. No. 23 231   Printed in U.S.A